MEMPHIS

impressions

FARCOUNTRY
PRESS

photography by **Bob Schatz**

Right: The iconic B. B. King's Blues Club sign beckons music lovers.

Far right: The Children's Museum of Memphis entices youngsters to explore their imaginations through inviting hands-on exhibits.

Title page: Like Bourbon Street in New Orleans, Beale Street offers a colorful history. It was declared the Home of the Blues by an Act of Congress on December 15, 1977.

Front cover: A fiery sunset silhouettes the aptly nicknamed M Bridge.

Back cover: Two hip Elvises take a break on Beale Street.

ISBN 10: 1-56037-427-6
ISBN 13: 978-1-56037-427-5

© 2009 by Farcountry Press
Photography © 2009 by Bob Schatz

Above, left: Visitors to Memphis can take in the city's sights the old-fashioned way: from a seat on the Main Street Trolley.

Above, right: The Mud Island Monorail provides great views of the downtown skyline, the broad Mississippi River, and Mud Island River Park.

Facing page: The exquisite China exhibit is one of the most popular at the Memphis Zoo, which occupies seventy-six acres in Overton Park and features more than 3,500 animals.

Above, left: Located in the heart of downtown Memphis, AutoZone Park opened in 2000 and is home to the Memphis Redbirds, AAA Minor League affiliate of the St. Louis Cardinals. PHOTO COURTESY OF MEMPHIS CONVENTION AND VISITORS BUREAU.

Above, right: Located on historic Beale Street, the Memphis Rock 'n' Soul Museum chronicles the dazzling sounds that have made the city famous.

Right: On a clear evening the Memphis Redbirds challenge the Oklahoma Redhawks at spacious AutoZone Park.

Above, left: Spring provides a backdrop for an architectural feature of St. Peter Catholic Church, built in 1855.

Above, right: Visitors to the National Ornamental Metal Museum can stroll through the sculpture garden and observe artists at work.

Left: Fans of the NBA's Memphis Grizzlies cheer their team in the state-of-the-art FedEx Forum, located near Beale Street. The team relocated from Vancouver in 2001.

Above, left: Sun Studio became legendary when Elvis Presley crooned his first recording there. Icons such as Johnny Cash, Jerry Lee Lewis, and Carl Perkins started in this studio as well.

Above, right: The Fire Museum of Memphis celebrates the history and heroism of local firefighters, educating visitors with displays of historic firefighting equipment and other interactive exhibits.

Facing page: Visitors come to Sun Studio's souvenir shop and soda fountain for memorabilia, treats, and to reminisce about the early days of rock and roll.

Above, left: Modern lines mark the Memphis Public Library, which greeted patrons for the first time in 2001.

Above, right: Noted for its unique water features, the Mid-America Mall on Main Street is one of the nation's longest pedestrian malls.

Right: Works displayed in the galleries of the National Ornamental Metal Museum range from jewelry to sculpture to architectural ironwork; the museum includes historic as well as contemporary metal objects.

Above: Tours of the Gibson Guitar Factory allow visitors a glimpse at the intricate process of guitar-making that has shaped the music world for more than 100 years. The artisans who craft the instruments are called luthiers.
PHOTO COURTESY OF MEMPHIS CONVENTION AND VISITORS BUREAU.

Left: A youngster points out an object of interest across the expansive Mississippi.

Above, left and right: Elvis Presley fans from around the world make pilgrimages to Graceland, once the legend's home and now a museum. Presley is buried on the estate.

Facing page: The Memphis College of Art attracts students studying graphic design, painting, photography, printmaking, animation, and other visual arts.

Above, left: Music fans spend hours browsing the selections in Pop Tunes, a music store Elvis often frequented as a teenager.

Above, right: Stax Records began as a small record store in a small theater and grew into one of the most important recording studios in the nation, launching the careers of such artists as Isaac Hayes, Otis Redding, and Wilson Pickett. Now the Stax Museum of American Soul, the facility pays tribute to the birth of soul music.

Left: The Stax Museum of American Soul offers a look at more than 2,000 items of memorabilia, ranging from album covers and rare photos to Tina Turner's gold-sequined stage dress and Isaac Hayes's restored, peacock-blue 1972 Superfly Cadillac El Dorado.

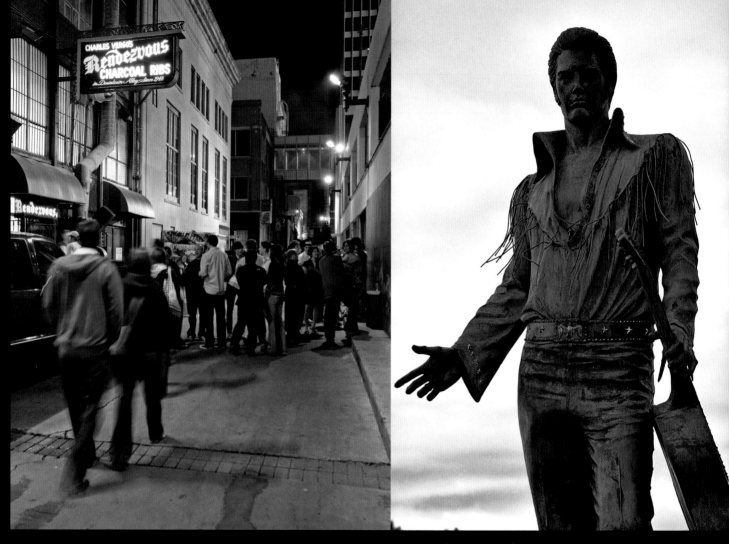

Above, left: The slow-cooked ribs at Charles Vergo's Rendezvous make the wait worthwhile.

Above, right: A statue of the King striking his signature pose, on Beale Street.

Facing page: Street musicians sing the blues on Beale Street, a tradition that defined the area since the early twentieth century.

Above, left: Court Square provides a quiet retreat from busy downtown.

Above, right: Many Memphians stop to admire *Without Boundaries*, a captivating solar-system creation by Yvonne Bobo in Peabody Park.

Right: The Four Seasons Garden's fountain offers a focal point for this attractive part of the ninety-six-acre Memphis Botanic Garden.

Above: Earth's past springs to life through the fossils and displays in the Pink Palace Museum's natural history exhibit.

Above: Who knows what intriguing piece of art will emerge from the industrial workshops at the National Ornamental Metal Museum.

Above: The Arcade Restaurant, a fixture of downtown Memphis, serves its patrons hearty fare. Established in 1919, the Arcade is said to be Memphis's oldest restaurant.

Left: The unique Crystal Shrine Grotto, a manmade cave located in Memorial Park Cemetery, was created by Mexican folk artist

Above, left: Folks in Memphis enjoy nice weather while dining al fresco along the Main Street Trolley Line.

Above, right: Although the Dixon Gallery and Gardens began in 1976 with a small collection, its impressive museum and grounds now contain more than 2,000 works of art.

Left: The Memphis Cotton Exchange, founded in 1874, showcases the trade that was once vital to the regional economy. The history of the cotton trade is explored through an on-site museum. In its heyday, Memphis was the largest port on the Mississippi River between St. Louis and New Orleans.

THE PRODUCERS
THRU JULY 27
SASON SPONSOR
DR THOMAS RATLIFF

PLAYHOUSE

Above: Since it began entertaining Memphians in 1936, the Levitt Shell has seen such performers as Elvis Presley, Johnny Cash, the Grateful Dead, and many other musical greats. It is located in lush Overton Park. ROBERT WILLIAMS PHOTO.

Facing page: The popular Playhouse on the Square has expanded numerous times since its inception and provides Memphis with a professional resident theater company.

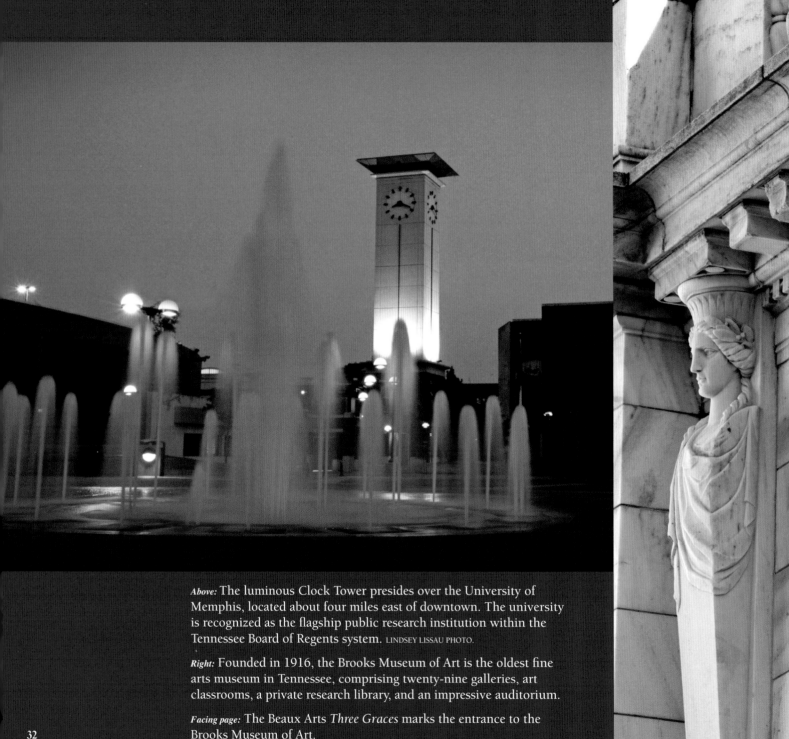

Above: The luminous Clock Tower presides over the University of Memphis, located about four miles east of downtown. The university is recognized as the flagship public research institution within the Tennessee Board of Regents system. LINDSEY LISSAU PHOTO.

Right: Founded in 1916, the Brooks Museum of Art is the oldest fine arts museum in Tennessee, comprising twenty-nine galleries, art classrooms, a private research library, and an impressive auditorium.

Facing page: The Beaux Arts *Three Graces* marks the entrance to the Brooks Museum of Art.

Left: Nearly five times the size of Central Park, 4,500-acre Shelby Farms Park is home to more than twenty bodies of water, multi-use trails, sports fields, an amphitheater, and even a herd of American bison. Originally the site served as the Shelby County Penal Farm; prison inmates produced food for other inmates and jail staff.

Below: Mud Island River Park, which opened to the public in 1982, includes a museum, restaurants, and an amphitheater. Its River Walk includes a five-block-long representation of the lower Mississippi River, which provides historical and geological information about this stretch of the waterway.

Above, left: One of two giant pandas at the Memphis Zoo peers out from its home at the China exhibit.

Above, right: The Peabody Hotel is best known for its March of Ducks tradition, which dates back to the 1930s. The famous Peabody ducks live on the hotel roof and march to the fountain in the lobby at 11 A.M. daily, much to the delight of visitors.

Facing page: Designed in the Italian Renaissance style, the Peabody Hotel was built in 1925 by Robert Brinkley, who sought to create an oasis of elegance. CBS once broadcast weekly from the historic hotel's Skyway Ballroom on the top floor.

Above, left: With its twenty-three specialty gardens, including this Japanese Garden of Tranquility, the Memphis Botanic Garden is a haven inside Audubon Park.

Above, right: This beautifully detailed bronze fountain graces Court Square.

Right: The Lichterman Nature Center is an arboretum and education center that includes an underwater viewing area, a three-story forest boardwalk, and more.

Above, left: At 418 feet in length and featuring 222 staterooms, the *American Queen* is the largest steamboat ever built.

Above, right: It began as a one-room log cabin, but Davies Manor Plantation expanded from the 1830s until 1950. Today the restored property offers a glimpse of pioneer life.

Facing page: Fans of John Grisham's Memphis-based novels are already familiar with the Shelby County Courthouse, which occupies a full city block downtown.

Above: In addition to its barbecued ribs, the Blues City Cafe offers fried catfish, tamales, and charbroiled steaks. Nightly live entertainment draws a crowd.

Right: W. C. Handy, who wrote the song "Beale Street Blues," is commemorated in a life-sized bronze statue on Beale Street. Known as the Father of the Blues, Handy was instrumental in the development of the "contemporary" turn-of-the-century style that came to be known as Memphis blues.

Above: The Brooks Museum of Art's permanent collection includes works by modern artists as well as the Kress Collection of Renaissance paintings and artwork by Pierre-Auguste Renoir, Winslow Homer, and noted regional artist and former Memphis resident Carroll Clear.

Above: From its humble beginnings in 1986, Memphis Motorsports Park has established itself as one of the most popular racing venues in the country, hosting more than 200 events a year. The complex features a three-quarter-mile NASCAR track in addition to an NHRA championship drag strip. PHOTO COURTESY OF MEMPHIS CONVENTION AND VISITORS BUREAU.

Right: Surrounded by a Victorian-era neighborhood, six-acre Morris Park gives locals a place for urban recreation.

Above, left: An ocelot returns a visitor's inquisitive stare with a steady gaze of its own at the Memphis Zoo.

Above, right: Built in 1890 with an eclectic blend of architectural styles, the Tennessee Club was once a hub for business and political activity.

Right: The Railroad Bridge is just one example of urban renovation in the historic Cooper-Young neighborhood.

Above, left: Water splashes over the World Fountain in the gardens of the Dixon Gallery and Gardens, known for its Impressionist and Post-Impressionist collections.

Above, right: Parked in front of Graceland, Elvis Presley's legendary 1955 Pink Cadillac Fleetwood sedan was a gift to his mother, Gladys, who, ironically, never owned a driver's license. USED BY PERMISSION, ELVIS PRESLEY ENTERPRISES, INC.

Facing page: Fountains make for a grand entrance to the Mid-America Mall, a popular place for both shopping and people watching.

Above, right: An experienced pit-master patiently tends the fare at the Cozy Corner Barbecue Restaurant.

Above, left and facing page: Shoppers browse through the wares at A. Schwab's, established in 1876 and run by the same family for generations. The motto of the store: "If you can't find it at A. Schwab's, you're better off without it!"

Above, left and right: The spacious grounds of Overton Park provide ample opportunities for enjoying the outdoors, from golfing to picnicking.

Facing page: A bold, red Japanese-style bridge punctuates the study in greens at the Memphis Botanic Gardens.

Above, left: The Woodruff-Fontaine House, a beautiful French Victorian mansion completed in 1870 along what was then called Millionaires' Row, is now open for tours by the public. The museum's collection includes period furniture as well as Victorian clothing.

Above, right: Featuring an ornate terra-cotta façade, the Kress Building was completed in 1927.

Left: Construction on the Cathedral of Immaculate Conception was completed during the Great Depression; it was dedicated in 1938.

Above, left: Visitors can take a scenic tour of the city in a horse-drawn carriage.

Above, right: A funky work of art invites visitors to check out one of the trendy art galleries along the South Main Historic Arts District.

Facing page: In Memphis, May means it's time for the World Championship Barbecue Cooking Contest. Hundreds of teams compete for prizes— and bragging rights. Memphians also enjoy the samplings from a variety of vendors at the fair.

Above, left: The 1929 Hickman Building in downtown Memphis is on the National Register of Historic Places.

Above, right: Built in 1930 and rising twenty-nine stories, the Sterick Building is one of the city's tallest structures.

Left: Despite its name, Presidents Island was once home to gamblers, a penal farm, and yellow-fever refugees. It is now a thriving industrial district.

Above: The aromas are savory and the competition is stiff during the annual World Championship Barbecue Cooking Contest.

Left: Burkle Estate, a historic home built in 1849 by a German immigrant, is believed to have been an important stop on the Underground Railroad, helping slaves escape north and providing safety through a series of interconnected tunnels that eventually led to the Mississippi River.

Above, left: The Memphis City Beautiful Commission, formed in 1930 and the oldest beautification commission in the United States, occupies the historic Massey-Schaeffer home on Adams Avenue.

Above, right: Barge-tows such as this one serve as a reminder that the beautiful Mississippi River is also a busy workplace for many Tennesseans.

Right: Part of the University of Memphis, the Chucalissa Archaeological Museum includes an archaeological park that was established to train scientists and educate the public. Chucalissa is dedicated to exploring the lives and history of regional Native Americans.

Above, left: Commercial businesses along Main Street.

Above, center: Woodruff-Fontaine House features period furnishings, allowing visitors to step back in time to the Victorian era.

Above, right: A fiddle evokes an evening of music around the fire at the Davies Manor Plantation.

Facing page: Located within walking distance of Beale Street and other landmarks, the Inn at Hunt Phelan is a restored 1828 antebellum mansion that offers lodging and fine dining.

Above: Memphis wouldn't be Memphis without barbecue. With a reputation for great food and friendly service, Neely's has served up regional fare since the late 1980s. PHOTO COURTESY OF NEELY'S BARBECUE

Right: A landmark at the north end of downtown Memphis, the Great American Pyramid was modeled after the Pyramid of Cheops in Egypt. The 321-foot-tall structure encloses a stadium with seating for 22,000.

Above and left: A solemn monument to the tragic day in 1968 when Martin Luther King, Jr., was assassinated, the Lorraine Hotel is now the site of the National Civil Rights Museum, which chronicles African-American history from slavery to the present.

Above, right: Musician W. C. Handy lived in this small house when he composed "Memphis Blues" and "St. Louis Blues." The charming structure is now the W. C. Handy Home and Museum, which traces the history of Memphis blues.

Above: Time is always of the essence for FedEx; Memphis is the express mail firm's corporate headquarters.

Left: Hoping for his big break, a street musician entertains pedestrians on Beale Street. Performers have worked this 1.8-mile stretch since the 1860s.

Above: Founded in 1848, Rhodes College is a four-year liberal arts school with an enrollment of approximately 1,700. Thirteen of its Gothic buildings are on the National Register of Historic Places.

Right: Rhodes College president William E. Troutt engages a student in discussion.

Facing page: The two-acre Cancer Survivors Park, which opened in 2008, features a sculpture by Mexican artist Victor Salmones of eight life-sized people passing through a rectangular maze that symbolizes the disease.

Left: In 1930, Clyde Parke began carving this miniature circus, which ultimately took thirty years to complete. Featuring moving acrobats, a marching band, spectators, and more, Clyde Parke's Miniature Circus is on exhibit at the Pink Palace Museum.

Below: Entertainer Danny Thomas founded the St. Jude Children's Research Hospital in 1962 as a place for children with devastating diseases to receive treatment regardless of their families' ability to pay. PHOTO COURTESY OF ST. JUDE CHILDREN'S RESEARCH HOSPITAL.

Above: From 1949 to 1953, Elvis Presley and his parents, Gladys and Vernon, lived in apartment 328 at Lauderdale Courts. Saved from demolition in the 1980s, Lauderdale Courts is now Uptown Square, a mixed-income apartment community in downtown Memphis. Today, visitors can stay in the Elvis Suite, which re-creates what the Presley home may once have looked like. PHOTO COURTESY OF ALLEN MIMS/THE UPTOWN PARTNERSHIP.

Left: This early mansion now houses the Memphis Theological Seminary of the Cumberland Presbyterian Church.

Above: A blues fan might pick up a recording of W. C. Handy's 1912 classic "Memphis Blues" from this Beale Street retailer.

Left: The Frisco, Harahan, and Memphis-Arkansas bridges are built side by side at a point where the Mississippi narrows. Memphis is the second-largest cargo port on the river.

During his twenty-five years as a commercial photographer, **Bob Schatz** has produced photographs for numerous publications, including *Elle, Forbes, Fortune, National Geographic Traveler, The New York Times Magazine, Newsweek,* and *PC Week.*

Over the years, Schatz has won numerous awards and commissions for his fine art prints, which have been exhibited around the country. His photographs are part of permanent collections at the Cheekwood Fine Arts Center, the Frist Center for the Visual Arts, the Metro Nashville Arts Commission, the Nashville Public Library, and the Tennessee State Museum. His portfolio can be viewed online at www.stockschatz.com.